COME TO TOWER

Special Thanks

Thank you for believing in me!

Alan Tsang, Craig Mush, Ash Gray, Safak Bozkurt, Planet Zogg family, Sarah Holman, Aidan English and Lauren Penhaligon, Amy Chamberline, Avital Raz, Gamze Yavuz Ugurlu, Rich Orange Whitehead & Deborah Mahmoudieh, Tony & Saskia &Rabish Robots. Rafiki Jazz family, Kat Harrison, Trystan Morris, Marcus Abbott, Magdalena, Gozde Ozdemir, my Process Engineering professor - your Pirate Aysegul here, and my brother Koray Balkose.
Thank you for protecting; my mother Leyla Balkose, my grandmother Usulet Sengolge, all my uncles and aunties, my cousins.
And my dad, Omer Balkose.

COME TO TOWER

By Ayse Balkos

Each poem is a song

For some OF US It was difficult For some time

BEST MELODIES

The Best melodies are yet to be sung
Best melodies are hanging on my tongue
Best melodies are yet to be found
Best melodies are coming out of my lungs
Best melodies are the ones
you hold in your mouth
Best melodies are touched with your sight
Best melodies are given with your heart
Best melodies are crowned in the night

OPEN YOUR HEART

Sit in front of me
It is time to have a chat about stuff
Why did you, why did you leave me?
I have just loved you so much!
And he raised his immaculate glassy
fingers
his eye brows
his eyes
And said

I promise
Open your heart

BEAUTIFUL

It is time to make that conversation
to move on to our lives
Not to be a rag at somebody else's under foot

I thought
you were gonna stay with me!
Because you were holding me

But now,
I've been so alone
you left without a word
I just felt so alone in this whole world
Why?

He nods his head Time to time
Its been so quiet

I thought I understood some of me
When I finished the conversation with me
I climbed, climbed
Climbed over the hills

The time was flickering
It was advancing on my feet

The time was flat
When I had no money
I walked the 5 miles

I raised my eyebrows
He said
It's just not about somebody loves you
It's about you love yourself
        You are so beautiful
that is why I can still feel the love
        radiating from you
I can feel everything
you have buried in your silence
You need to send your eyes
to the depths of your heart
In that darkness
Find that flickering light of moon
Behind that is sun

I LOOSE MYSELF

Ageing in the ageless times
What was the name I was given
To unfold this mime
I've had many more
Since the days of me
in my slow shores
I was a different woman then
Wearing much the same clothes
I was born into
I am bigger, brighter,
mountains lighter next to you
Everyday
I dream about this moment
Everyday I loose myself around you
I am not a gambler, battler
A wrestler, hustler, scrambler
Things are moving so much faster
Like a flash-light on a subway door
I don't want this dark clouds
over my head any more
I was given a name so long ago
What was it
Since then I used many more

Things are moving
Faster, slower
Still learning to walk on curbed roads
                last modified myself this morning
How lucky I am,
I am in love with you
Diamonds are hanging on my door
Everyday
I loose myself around you
                Everyday

EVERLASTING

Is casting ever lasting
Is there everlasting
Have we got a caver
Are you paving
Are we raving
I am craving
I've been shaving
Here is my savings
There is graving
We're time saving
Stay with me
Is living forgiving
Mis-giving at thanks-giving
There is glazing and raising
and phrasing and praising
Also star gazing Life is amazing
Self-raising donuts like
Double glazing
Its warm and hot
I'm rising, uprising, surprising,
enterprising, improvising
They are advertising

Uncompromising
Enchanting Dismounting
Erecting and distracting
Exactly overacting
Effecting, respecting, expecting,
self-respecting, unsuspecting
We're courting, supporting, sorting, sporting
Jotting, knotting, potting, nodding,
Transporting
I am closing, even snoozing
Off dozing in housing
Un-confusing and amusing
Children!
Take of your shirts
Take of your trousers
It is playtime!
Are we raving
Are we craving
Are we saving
Are we shaving
Are we raving
Are we engraving
Are we time saving
Are we slaving

Are we ironing
Are we serving
Are we nerving
Are we swearing
Are we deserving
Are we deserting
Are you casting, even lasting
Are we blasting,
contrasting,
accounting
Is life everlasting

COME TO TOWER

I hear a voice calling
Coming from the ether
Its like from nowhere
There is a tower apparently,
waiting for me
I can hear its calling
My individuality
I listen to myself
I am embracing
I say I can do better
I've just lost in my thought
I hold onto my mould
on the road reward
I gave up the sword
People think
I kick, sneak I am thick
In my backyard I pick up the lick
I'm allotropically and
categorically maverick
I hear a voice calling me from ether
It's like
somewhere out of nowhere
The world is homeric, heroic

Sometimes I feel like hanging around
Sometimes yinging and yanging
In reality
I love jazzing
I thrive in painting
I hear a voice calling me
There is a road to follow, it says
And I follow
There is this game I play
its called Morality
devotees
The good and the evil
in the garden of Eden
It stars the serpent, Adam and Eve,
God and tree of life and
tree of knowledge
And all characters are me
I am on the road
I follow the trail
I hear a voice calling me
It is embracing
The road beneath my feet is blossoming
I've just lost in my thought
Reward
I gave up the sword

BE CURIOUS

Trust your addict instinct
Be authentic, surrender,
ready to do the dirty work
Be curious
Don't be brain washed
Face with your fears
Change your narrative
Find a quest to follow
Believe you are gold
Count, convert, exchange
This is not negotiable
It is important
where you are coming from you think,
but It's not
What matters is
The new stage you enter
where you are heading towards
Be authentic, surrender
Ready to do the dirty work
I don't know what tomorrow brings
When you have or
don't have anything
But family is the thing
you want to have

Make it
or
I am giving you Take it
Be the centre of your own brick
you inhabit
Everyone will be welcoming
Cover the bruises
Be gentle and be antiseptic
Get out of your own way darling
Your guns are not good to hold onto
Heads up
The come down is real
Be authentic, surrender
Get your finger tips in the dark soil
Create one thing
you can be good at
Love and study history
Catch a rainbow
Have the moon,
watch the water fall
Be Curious
Find a goal that is worth of your soul
Every time
everybody has a crime scene to run
I carried bags of weed

in the boot of my car many times
stood on an inch away
from killing someone
In the name of freeing myself
With a knife
There is no jokes in this life
This is serious business living
The system is system
It ain't gonna change
It is you who I care
Use what you have to protect yourself
Don't rush
Hold on to your emotions
Express them in a way
to make something good out of yourself
Self control is the key to the maturity
To reach out every goal you have
I care about you
I know how your heart is pure
Explosions to every injustice!
To fix your anger,
to prove your worth
You shout louder
That's not how it works
Your silence has your plot

Be wise, use your brain
One more thing Remember
An addict is an addict
Anger, cocaine, tobacco,
sugar or alcohol
All comes from the same empty feeling
It is the void you inhabit
Study your mind and your heart
Be curious
Remember to be gentle to your soul
Be tough too your body
It is how we grow
Don't be brain washed
Face with your fears
Change your narrative
Find a quest to follow
Believe you are gold
You are gold

LIONESTIE

So I told myself
Don't lash yourself
Only a fool
looks for a food in a cage
by a gate
By the scorpion cave
The allegory of cave, hey!
There was a time
I was a woman of 35
Beautiful from inside and out
People looked at me as if
I was tossing around
As if I was dossing
Because I had nowhere
to sleep in happy, calm
You know the feeling of warmth
inside and out
Along with a candle light
I saw a lion in me and called it
Lionestie
She growled and said
Don't run this time
Sun is swift

When those shades wrap your legs
You feel shaky from shady
Don't run this time
There will be nobody coming to
rescue you if you run
Stay within yourself
as such in your home
You give yourself a comb
To dust yourself off
from your scorn
with a smile
A green license to be happy
A mask to be masked
by other masks
A green grind by groins of other tasks
She said,
I am a Lionestie,
the lion of esteem!
They said
Run
She said
Don't
There is only your legs
to take you to a silent comfort

Go slow!

FUCK YOU TERRY

I am opposed to ruling authority
all over me
They measure, mark, dart,
count me
in their list of slavery
Hope is a deadly road
Zealotry is a theory
On citizenry
He checked me back then
Slacked me
Sacked me back then
Hold me
What are you doing tonight then?
I am a gemstone
Balancing on a curb stone
Hitting on another milestone
I was listening to Huckleberry
Walking along
a breezy rocky Island
with my mate Terry
Drinking sherry
just had some hot curry
I was sweating
He tried to make me feel guilty,

sorry
That day is a bit blurry, slurry
My head has gone fizzy
I am not to be added
in your chickens inventory
Terry, Terry!
Where are you Terry?
He lives at top of the hills of Shrewsbury
Fuck you, Terry!

LOVE SONG

This is gonna be a love song
The way my gut petrified,
quantified
The radio sings
Its alright, Its alright
Its alright Bob!
Sitting along with
a pen and a notebook
All I need to hear
was a polka dot song
Wild in the bushes
Little shrubs intertwine my arms
It's alright
This is gonna be a love song
Hold on!
Bob on the radio says,
its alright
It is all over
no time to sour our casts
Some regrets
crawling at their bests
I laughed
I thought about you Bob

The way you felt
When you left,
when you said
It's alright
Think about this Bob,
A kitten in a mitten
in a nighty smitten
Warm and cosy
Kitten rolls softly
Pursy, curly, furry
I caught the paw,
My face
Dropped
Hold on
Its not finished yet
Crawl crawl crawl
kitten on a roll
Roll roll
With a paw soft on a gondola
It puffed my ears
Like an owl
I thought about you Bob
The way you felt
When you left when you said
Its alright

Think about this, Bob!
You are my moon,
I am your sun
We shine in each other’s gown
Hold on
This is gonna be a love song

GREATEST SCULPTURE

He took his hammer
He knocked down his two front teeth
After the prayers and hymns
At the chapel of his wedding
He watched
Lucy and Ann playing
You got to go
Come on
You got to go
Before they come inside
The windows are open
A door ajar
For Lucy and Ann
Before they come back
Its time to go
And he's gone!
He pulled on his jacket
He stuck back his hair
To make a life of his dreams
He burned Lucy and Ann's
Greatest sculpture ever live

GYMNASTING

Fly like a bird they say
Be a bird they say
They do
And you fly
Free from managing your life
They say
But Why?
You don't need to manage your life
You're just gonna gonna
drift along with
What they say...
Do that say
Do what they say
You see
If I don't have the words in front of me
I just can't say them out load
I've been flying like a bird
As the way they've told me to do
I am growing some wings
Like angel wings
dropped from the heaven
This earth is heaven
Just listen to your own mind

You can do, whatever it takes!
Then I think to myself
Wouldn't that be a great surprise
to everyone
If I become someone
Like an gymnast Coexisting
Like an observant, snowcat or
iconoclast
I don't know that word
I've just made it up
so I can sound a bit cool
I come for a chat with you today
I asked
What do you want?
What do you want in this life?
And you said!
I don't know
I am just Gymnasting
Inconsistently
I am co-existing
Its about the change
I am giving you some wings to fly
I think myself is a little confused
I'm Just close to madness
What looks like

one thing
      Is maybe another
So I have to remind myself
about the life
of that
Big orange circle in the sky
Called Sun!

I DO KNOW

I don't want to say
I don't know any more
Because I do know
I just don't know what others know
I don't know what they think
But I know what they feel
I feel the feel of the feelings
        I feel my love
I feel your love
The silent love
It was raining outside
it was so sunny inside
I was covered with scarf
It was hot and steaming
I was feeling this thing!
I knew we only had just
five minutes
        Maybe two
        Maybe thirty sec
That twenty meters long scarf
You became the scarf
It was hot in there
I can't untangle myself

God help me what would I do
I am just statueing
        I am not lazing
        I am just feeling of the feeling
I became me, just me, simply me
In me, I had another me
I carried with me
And that me stood there with you
For a split second
I just wanted to tell you
Before I saw you
I knew I was with you
I melted like ice cream
Like snow on top of mountains
In the Mediterranean seaside
        It wasn't white
        It doesn't have to be pure
It doesn't have to have colour
Because I'm blind
I only feel the things

BEING ME IS STRANGE TODAY

No
Not today
Nothing special
Don't feel like it
Being me is strange today
I don't feel like being me today
End has no logic
Or the beginning
Discovering the will
Taking my cat out for a walk
It's just, you know the look
Expectations, ha
I don't feel like going to my allotment
Digging the soil
Checking on the gate
That thing is solid
Something nice
Like drawing chalks
Lines
Red, blue, yellow, black
It dissolves
The woman cleaning the window
Hard

I don't feel like
taking my ideas and thoughts for a
walk
    Today
I don't feel like being me
    Today

RUSSIAN ROULETTE

One two three four
ten thousand or more
Nibbling zigging giggling
Add to the joy of rising
Would I pull the trigger
Don't force it to know
Don't force it
I'm athletic
I am playing Russian with you
In the scissors of your mind
We are ready for each other
Resurrection 'round the corner
Hope is round like Russian Roulette
        To my own spinner
I kiss the devil from his tongue
Catching and chaining my neck
        to the elephant
Devil's ride is unforeseeable
Light is in the black hole
Wild hearts making love songs
Singing heart songs
Sing songs
Light is in the black hole

I am a dream of yours
A dream applause
A dream of course
A dream resourced
Overdraws and melancholy of yours
If you abandon your dream
In the valley of the lily
It will turn into a sour,
        crappie ,sweaty,
        eerie thingy
Not harmoniously
Giving the smell of a bad breath
In a love spell of Rasputin
The gates are wide open

MONKEY

Show me a monkey dance
Give me a monkey ass
Wiggle wiggle wiggle monkey
Dance for me
Wiggle wiggle for me
So the monkey wants to fuck with me!
Hey! Can you handle me
Bananas and monkey nuts
That’s it my lovely
Show me what a good monkey
Jerry Kane
Hurricane
That's the monkey’s name
I am a sealer on the wall
I am a dealer in the hall
I am the saviour of your soul
Monkey dance for me
If you play around
You will pay for it
If you turn around
You will see me
I am everywhere
when there’s nothing else to cry

I am the real witch
I teach how to kill to Kill Bill,
Monkey!

MY HUSBAND

Keep on the same road
When you're on your way to here
Cut your coat to a size
I could wear
Take no risks on your way my
husband!
Come from the green hills

MY VICES

My Vices My advisers
I hear a voice calling me
Come to tower with me
I gave birth to the tower
In the kingdom of the Sun God
Coronation, here is my nectar
        I gave birth to the tower
        In the 5 foot under ground
I am playing happy, feeling hungry
What the voices are offering me
My vices are giving advices
in the dark night
Voices are calling me
        Come to tower with me
Friction on fraction
The energy explosion
My vices are advising me
to take actions
The darkness gave birth to me
        Now here, here and now
And now

I am giving birth back to myself
In the darkness of this
sticky floored night
Come to tower with me

COBRA

What do you do
When you're born
When you try to reach that One
What do you do
When you cry
When your cry doesn't reach out life
There is no meaning of saying
what they'r saying
When the saying means nothing
The profit is sailing, nailing
Because the prophet is oily grailing
Write this down
I survived the trip I was on
The trip that brutalised my bones
Did I eat the stay alive
To say,
I was alive
I am a Cobra
What do you do when you'r born
On a page you don't belong
Finger prints all over you

When you fight the way I do
In this armour,
I fight like cobra
Not a tiger in water
Not an old soldier
I have got my grip on this rota
Let me chat you
Let me die if I lie
Do I sound pretentious?
Its chivy eye
Or something like
My destiny is written on a hook
In this armour
I am a cobra
Make no bones in this theatre
My temple
Not a phase
This multi face
Looking for a catch phrase
in this rat race
Mother, father, terrain I obtained
not the same

Let me die if I lie
When you fight
to get out of this water
When those tigers
looking around
You make fun of me
Don't care what you think of me
What I think is
what will I become of me
From Kansas City Missouri
To the world
My words will go ahead of me
With my Ashes next to my hand
I beat the rat race
My mother, my father?
With my voice
I go further than I dream of me

FOR NO REASON

We live for no reason
The vibrations of this new
segmentation
Is a prediction of the upcoming
expedition
Ex played an addition in my education
Life is a dramatisation of my actions
What you hear here is
The footsteps of habitual Titan
Walking away from her segregation
To be united with her coalition
To end the days of demoralisation
Get yourselves warm seats
Honey due beasties
I am head-charged, gate-crashed
Glued to secret-garden
Enough
When you're ready
Stir me
Uncover me
Savour the brave in me
Remove the lid, turn up the heat
Taste to see if you want more of me

Fill your hands with me
Drink the cup Full of me
Just before resting in me
Favour the brave in me
Strongly believe in me
Honest revolution needs no apology
Thicken the thief
Be imminent
Rip it up now I am up now
Enough is enough now
I am not wounded, shredded
You, back off now
I don't get into conflict for no reason
Fire drawn to me
Fire melts the metal in me
For no reason, you push
I push back for no reason
The law of reaction is for no reason
Stir me every now then
Take the lid off me
Fill your pot with me
Spread me over the beastie
Waters are boiling
Pre-heated oven
All for no reason

TOO EARLY

Baby, it's too early
Never to live, never to run
Never to forget,
life is just a bit of fun
Forgive, forget, give and take
Like a freshly eaten raw fruit cake
Love is a sight on a kite
I am not ready to take it
I am in a fight
I love being loved
Love being love
Love is is all there is
Baby love me
I am not ready to fight
Having a bit, this, that
Growing rules of the world is confusing
Emotions are attractions
I don't care about the elections
The ships, the bombs, shell drops T
he war in my heart is cold
For freedom of the life I live in bare
On benefits, artificial supplies,
nutritions

Never to live
Never to run
Never to forget
I see
        The gaze
        The silence of my
        knuckles
        behind this pace
In between two yellow lanes

PITCH DARK

I relaxed my jaw bone
In down town
Topped up, hyped up
This mighty Sheffield town
is quite alright
Under the moonlight,
Respect the Shema
The world tried to crash me,
cash me, flat me, tire me
Now they want to rehire me
What the fuck?
I know nothing
I know what is an unknown,
I am the unknown
Know this in this tone,
I don't care about your unknown
My unknown is better for me
I am the one who seeks the light
Night after night
I carry a torch light for the full sight
It's white outside
Snow snow
Light light

I am the one who seeks the light
Night after night
My dreams are haunting
My nightmares are running like mares
I can't see a thing
The shiver is cascading
My legs are shaking,
Not working
I am running, flaming, firing, flaring
They are not caring
I am daring
My heart is racing, lacing
It is pitch dark, midnight
No moon light in sight
The steps are over flown
The darkness is behind
I am screaming, begging
It is creeping, scaring
There are people over there
I can see them
They can see me
They are watching
Seeing, hearing

But not moving even a toe
No-one is coming to
help me any time soon
I must keep going
It is muddy, muddy
Mud is slippery,
I am running, flying, slicing
The floor is sliding
Someone, something is chasing
It is my life
I am approaching
Pacing
The blood is spreading
Gentling warming, widening
My hair is moist
Sweat is cascading
My lungs are phlegming, outing
I see them
They can see me,
I can see them seeing me
They can hear me,
I am begging, Help me

I feel nothing
My limps are not working
My face won't be healing
any time soon
Keep running
I am not stopping
Darkness is chasing
Hold onto your guts baby

SALT

I started to begin to like you too
I have a feeling
How fucked you must be too
Salt salt every look is an assault
Do I look reckless?
Hey miss!
Do you want to give me your laces?
I'll take them under my braces
Keep me warm
itchiness of your graces
An orphan doesn't have a home
The streets don't welcome greasy
elbows
The charity that gives clarity away
Knowing a sick is like licking clay
I hear them
Isn't she disgusting
Who chooses to live like her
Sleeping on a mattress
Full of germs
I can't carry on looking at her
No offence
No homes, no phones

No jobs, no shower,
no clean clothes means no income
The more you fear
That fear penetrates to your bones
With the cold through your mould
You loose your peak, your height,
the tide
Salt salt every look is an assault
An orphan doesn't have a home
The streets don't welcome
The best is yet to come
I get a strap in my arm
Amputated my pump
I transform into a spoon diamond
I wear myself as a night gown
Have you swallowed a vibrator love
grinning like a Masketeer
Behind those cars
I started to begin like you too
I guess
I have a feeling
how fucked you must be too

SWALLOW IT

I get it
I lived every second, every moment of it
You don't see the woman
behind the stilted costume
She is too tall for you
to look deep into her eyes
She sees you, through
Swallow it I wrote it
You listen to it
Reaching an apogee
You bleach an apology
This is my creed
I am not quizzical I still love you
I am not egotistical
I have chosen to be evangelical
over diabolical
No one walking on the streets
No one looking into the breeze
Solemnity of this blood is not the seed
life is taking its name from a story
It was a quiet night
You heard me on the radio
told me it is iconic, angelic, poetic

Flourishingly gut ranging
You can'?t stop listening to it
You are loosing yourself in it
Who is written it?
Who?
Am I too tall, too short, too dark, too
fair
Too soon, too late, to be seen,
not to be seen
Too sexy, too dull, too fat, too slim for
it
Am I too humble to be regarded,
to be respected
To be talented, to be accepted for it?
Swallow it
I have written every word
with my heart in it
I am the driver in this play
I am here to claim my part in it

THE PROOF OF LOVE

Sit
I have something to tell you
Sit
I have something to show you
It’s my heart
I’ve opened it for you
This is my blood
I poured it for you
Future pressures Drop
Something ends Stop
Something begins
The proof of love
Here we come
We drop the sound
You sit I bake
We eat
Sit
I've got something for you
Sit
I’ve got something to tell you
Have this
I made a cake for you

Eat it
I put my dress on to look nice around
you
4000 degree Celsius
We bake our babies

SKYLARK

I fly high towards the light
Late at night
Like a skylark
I am not crazy
I am not sorry
I could have even driven a lorry
My eyes just went a bit watery
It has nothing to do with me
They are trying to put their shit on me
Being on the road is not voluntary
I am dealing with me
Eating carvery, Playing soldiery
I have taken archery
I am not hungry for your
bulklary, Burberry, burglary
I know running is not a strategy
I fly high towards the light
Late at night
I am a skylark

HOW MUCH DO I WORTH?

The wind fall is now
Strong gales are
Welcome to the temple of fortune
The wind fall is here
As I promised you yesterday
Wind fall is washing over my feet
On the shore
One more sleight to go
The white horses of high tides
their rains tight
lost legs are found
On a golden dust
Temple of fortune is in me
The question is
How much do I worth If you weigh me?

MY STORY

One day my father died
The grief turned my mother into
something different
She was scared
There were wolves outside
I wasn't allowed to be out
I made no friends here
That world was dangerous
Mum's voice spoke
Inside of my head
She was inside of my head
I dreamed leaving the house one day
Mum's words followed me everywhere
If I loved her
She said
I wouldn't go any where

WHAT I THINK ABOUT MYSELF

A roaming hen brings dirt to coo
With her feet, mum said
She said
red lipstick
made me look like a whore
Mum taught me what to think about
myself
inside I knew
I was a butterfly
So I surrounded myself
With flowers

THE FIELDS

I closed my eyes
I could see myself dancing In the fields
The world beneath my eyelids
Showed me a way to freedom
I saw my feet going
Down the steps
Like shadows on the end of sticks
Like being weightless in the sky
Clouds passed by my feet
I saw a wolf
I just pass by it
When I open my eyes
I was really there, in the fields

LIVING

Are you familiar with stones in rice
That's how life was

TURKISH COFFEE

My grandmother loved having an early morning
So I loved it too
What I loved the most was
Her fortune telling

THE BENCH

When I feel like it
I go and sit down on a bench
With a look I carry
Red sky, golden sun, wild flowers
There a star
Waits for the night
Look we are there now
Turning away from the crowd
Looking for this place to sit down
By knowing that I know none
I sing
I sing my heart
On an unknown bench
To the sea knows all
I sing
I sing one word at a time
With one hand
On my waist
I sing to the time

VOICES

In the afternoon
I listened to the sea cry
In the evening I listened to mum
She cried her lungs out
With rivers of her soul
She knew that I knew
That gave her no place to hide

UN-LISTENED

Do you know what happens
In between decisions
What forces cause someone
To leave her mother
Mum! Will you answer
I wish

COMA LEAVE

My dad was in coma
Story written by Homer
His name was Omer
Coma, leave
14th December 1982
A man left a family in anoma
Where is my home, mama?
Reaching out to Varna
Upon Nirvana
Watching us from Tucana
Oh please Brahma
I pray to Shema
Howling with trauma
Dad had tumour
He had an aroma
Developed haematology
One day he swept into coma
Just like that
He was thirty one then
I am fourth one now
I was two and a half!
Coma is still here
Looking over my shoulder

Sleep swept him away
My skin crawled a splash
His bravery moustache
rustled a hush
Mum was thirty
Men were asking, sniffing like
Dogs on a hunt
For an easy pray
Mum, please stop this crying
The sink was not drying
Her bed was salting
She was angry

She was grieving
Dark clouds were dancing
Nothing was lasting
I was missing, mis-living,
Filling inner void with
Carnivorous explosions
A hunger to anger
Anger was compulsive
I was tilted, filtered, kilted
Dad was murdered
Mum was salted
Where was the sunshine?
Dark clouds were weaving
I was lone-ing
I was boiling
This anger was lashing
My heat was rising
My body was rising
To have a chance to say
Good bye!

A DREAM IS BORN

This is my Dad
Or what is left from him to me
Since that day
Something became very wrong
About what I was, where I was, whom I was
Then things become quiet
For a while
Something else was telling me
Who I was, what I was and
where I was suppose to be
It became scary
I walked away alone
To find
A door, maybe
To another world

BUTTERFLY

Little by little I heard the sound
First from far away
In the wild
Then it leaped out of me
The most beautiful butterfly
And I remembered
Who I was What I was
Where I was supposed to be
Then it all came back
Their rules
How ugly I was I shook my head
Spread my long beautiful wings
upwards
I danced swirling
While butterflies flew all around me

LILAC

One
Your favourite colour is lilac
Here is a lilac car
Lilac money a lilac house
lilac heart
I paint everything to lilac for you
You will feel sick, don't you?
I asked you
How can you have a favourite colour
you answered
How can you forgive if you are flawless
Living in a lilac world
This is your world Lilac man, lilac
woman
Lilac neighbours, lilac streets, lilac cat
Lilac smiles
You are lilac
Kill lilac

DREAM RED

I weigh myself In a dream red
Scale showed
twenty less than sixty eight
In kilos
I dreamed an eleven pm
A ringing phone's
Dropping sound on a taxi floor
Layers of the morning
Through the opening of a window
my nails were resting
On the counter of
A lost property box
The red bricks of Club 60
Who talked to me with a voice
Of a horse
of an uncertainty of a loss
It nailed the rest of me
Down onto a wall
Where a lime green suitcase
and my soul
Rested in a dreamed red

ESCAPE

I escaped from the mountain
Where you touched me
I escaped from the mountain of
You
Are you ready to call?
Is this is?
This is it?
Dial my number 1235579
666
I tried to love me before
I felt the same way as I always do
Before the escape
Before you

FREAK SHOW

It's a freak show
Likeness like you and I
Are you ready to live
Welcome to life
Mama mama
Do I need a thing?
Do I need a shirt, food
Mama
It's a freak show
This life
I am a freak in a freak show
Like a criminal
Mama look into my eyes
Do you think I'm yours
The serpent, flame that grows
the will to belong
I am a freak in a freak show

GEISHA

I don't know how far
I've walked away from you
I don't know how far
I've looked away from you
What lies in between
the comings and the goings
Yes I slept with your brother,
your mother and your cousin
The buses were looking for a boss!
I am Geisha
I am the dance of the butterflies
I criss-cross in my flip flops
For a guest like you
In a shop like this
Poppy sloppy hoppy
Why not come under my wings?
If you a sloppy hoppy
Then come on top
Some like it hot
Some like it on the top

Some like to whip
Some like to be whipped up
I know what you want
I am Geisha
queen of the butterflies
I am gonna move you

GIVE ME YOUR MONEY

Give me your money
I wear McQueen
Give me your money
I live in the land of Queen
Let me tell you a story
I buried my mess, friends
I played the back-hand
Beaten the poverty
Seeded in my mother's womb
I was a woman in denial
Waking up my powers
I wanted success
As an instant fame
I now play a different game
Give me, give me, give me your money
Heiress of this throne
tears of my joy
Under this diamond globe
In the heart-beat of steel city
There, I live a different life
Footsteps arrived
Like an old day's clap

One woman dreamed
An empire built,
I am that
Who walks to the Stone Rose
Give me your money

MURDER

I am so nervous
I have murder in my mind
Run to the hills with me
I'll show you
Where I will bury the body
Good morning life
And
All things good

The End

Bio

Raised in Turkey, Aysegul studied chemical engineering, later continuing with a masters degree (MBA).

Ayse moved to Sheffield, UK in 2009 and started a new life|career dedicated to art that is not only a reflection of discovery but also spirit of healing.

You can support her work via
Paypal: aybalse@gmail.com

Milton Keynes UK
Ingram Content Group UK Ltd.
UKHW040311080224
437360UK00001B/23